Grace for the Wounded

A Daily Devotional for those in Recovery

EDDIE OLIVAS III

WESTBOW®
PRESS
A DIVISION OF THOMAS NELSON
& ZONDERVAN

WestBow Press books may be ordered through booksellers or by contacting:

WestBow Press
A Division of Thomas Nelson & Zondervan
1663 Liberty Drive
Bloomington, IN 47403
www.westbowpress.com
1 (866) 928-1240

ISBN: 978-1-4908-3311-8 (sc)
ISBN: 978-1-4908-3312-5 (e)

Library of Congress Control Number: 2014906198

Printed in the United States of America.

WestBow Press rev. date: 09/25/2014

Contents

AUTHORS NOTE

This small book (*Project Soul Care: A Devotional that Celebrates God's Grace and Redemptive Power to Those in Recovery*) is a daily devotional that is comprised of a collection of writings from "Project Soul Care". Project Soul Care is a daily inspirational that is e- mailed to hundreds daily. **Each daily devotional has three paramount themes: trusting in God's word, the importance of perseverance, and the power of God's word to transform both the mind and confounding circumstances so one can transcend to a higher calling.** Because I am both a chaplain and a clinician my orientation is very integrative, (mindful of one's spiritual interior and one's psychological welfare). This devotional has been mined from a heart that has experienced profound personal pain, and years of exposure to suffering which comes from providing direct care to innumerable individuals from all walks of life. I like to refer to this care as, "psychological CPR". Many of the individuals that I have counseled over the years have struggled with agonizing mental illness or persistent addiction; hence, I have integrated both my psychological insight, as well as, my pastoral experiences in hospital chaplaincy. Many of the following meditations will have a paramount theme of restoration and affirm self-care as it relates to recovery.

My wife and I pray that this devotional becomes a great encouragement to you as well as a catalyst for your spiritual development and your journey working with a truly challenging population.

Acknowledgments

My loving wife: Sally Olivas

This little devotional was written during a very stressful and pressing time in my life. This work was composed during my recovery from brain surgery- a long and arduous season in my life. During this time I was able to reflect and write this little book. I am deeply grateful for my wife's Sally's encouragement and contribution to this book, and her tireless effort to see me recover.

My treasured friend and supporter: Kevin Flynn PhD

Without the support and encouragement of my dear friend and colleague Kevin Flynn PhD this endeavor would not be imaginable.

My primary desire for this book is to provide both information about recovery and afford the reader with a 31 day devotional that will illuminate God's grace and redemptive power to transform hearts, through hopeless circumstances. May God richly bless you!

Dedicated to

those who continue to suffer from the disease of addiction

ABOUT THE AUTHORS

Eddie Olivas III

Eddie Olivas III is an experienced substance abuse professional and a Registered Marriage Family Therapist. He has over 25 years' of clinical experience working with individuals from all walks of life. He has devoted the past 25 years to helping individuals who have struggled with mental illnesses and various addictions. He received his education and training in the field of psychology and addiction studies at Azusa Pacific University, UCLA, and Graceland University in Independence, Missouri. Eddie graduated with a Masters of Arts in Clinical Psychology (Marriage and Family Therapy) and a Master of Arts in Organizational Management from Azusa Pacific University. He received his clinical training at some of Los Angeles's most prestige's substance abuse treatment centers and acute psychiatric hospitals. Eddie has provided counseling services to individuals in such varied environments as hospitals, clinics, and intensive residential treatment centers. He is double certified by as a substance abuse counselor through CAADAC and Briening Institute so as to provide substance abuse counseling in the state of California. Lastly, he is a volunteer hospital Chaplain, ordained minister and an Oblate who received training from The *Prince of Peace Abby, Oceanside CA*. His focus is in the area of behavioral health care, addiction studies, and studying the benefits of spirituality as it relates to human suffering. He has been married to his wife Sally for 25 years and has a son and daughter. He spends his leisure hiking, writing and consulting.

Special Contributions made by Sally V. Olivas

Sally Olivas's greatest role is that of Wife &Mother. She has been a devoted follower of Jesus Christ for over three decades, and has been active in many ministry endeavors concentrating on women's issues. She also has presented on such topics as *"The meaning of Suffering" and Transcending to find Meaning"* Presently, she is continuing in her career in telecommunications which has been marked by many awards, accolades and exemplary service.

A Prayer for Recovery and Restoration

Dear Heavenly Father, I present myself to you with all my difficulties and shortcomings, I pray that you alleviate my unhealthy cravings and my own self-will which continues to beset me from experiencing your peace and having a vibrant relationship with You.

As I lay my life down for your service I trust you can heal me and deliver me from myself and my own tendencies to self-destruct. Dear, Lord I know you are able, and you will never leave me nor forsake me. Please deliver me from my addiction and help me find my way to recovery

In Jesus Name, Amen!

A WORKING DEFINITION OF ADDICTION: A BIOLOGICAL-PSYCHOLOGICAL-SOCIAL, AND SPIRITUAL DISEASE

The definition of addiction is not as easy as many think to define. This is because of its complexity and the many areas it affects in a person's life. Never the less, I have employed the disease concept of addiction to explain and define addiction. This concept lends itself from the medical model because addiction is truly a disease and it can be defined as a "bio-psycho-social-spiritual disease. Below is a brief summary of each component:

The Biological Component: (A Brain Disease)

Based upon my many years of experience providing counseling services to a multitude of individual's struggling with addictions, I can honestly say addiction is a brain disease marked by impairment in one's neurobiological system, thought patterns, emotionality, relational styles and a serious void in one's spiritual interior . In other words, addiction entails an imbalance and impairment in the "a Bio-Psycho-Social and Spiritual aspect of a person's very being. Addiction is usually "kick started" by trauma or chronic stress. More often then not, it is trauma that jump starts the addiction and chronic stress becomes the "trainer" of the brain's amygdala to be routinely in flight or fight mode which subsequently keeps the addiction in process. With all substance abuse the brain become increasingly stress sensitive. Both factors tend to create an imbalance in the dopaminergic system which in turn, produces a serious state of discomfort (dis euphoria) throughout one's entire body. It is this state of discomfort that makes one very vulnerable to addiction because drug use and or behavioral addiction brings temporary relief at the expense of changing brain functioning. The quandary of this "relief" is that it does in fact bring a temporary relief but at a huge price- addiction changes the "configuration of the brain" (making it stress sensitive, often times indefinitely, and changing neurotransmission). Addiction often creates neurochemical imbalances that will eventually perpetuate the addiction in spite of the most painful consequences imaginable.

After drug use (alcohol included) and the effects of the drug wears of a state of dis euphoria (the anadonia factor) usually kicks in. It is during this time the brain is depleted from feel-good chemicals and a hedonic drive is sparked, which drives the addiction to a very dangerous stage that many in the field refer to as the "high jacked brain". Oddly, the brain's, pleasure center remembers the experience and effects of the drug. It leaves a distinct monogram- the release of a flood of the neurotransmitter dopamine in the nucleus accumbens, (a cluster of nerve cells lying underneath the cerebral cortex). This process is well documented and is almost universally accepted by neuroscientist in the field of addiction. When the pleasure center of the brain is taken over, the addict's life becomes most dire because nothing else will matter in the addict's life except finding relief through drug use or a process addiction. As one can conclude, addiction is largely a brain disease (that involves the nucleus accumbens, hippocampus, and "his dear friend the amygdala") yet addiction clearly has a psychological, social and spiritual component as well.

The Psychological Component of addiction:

The psychological aspect of addiction is primarily simple. The drug use will be perpetuated by the pleasures principle and justified by what experts refer to as denial mechanism. This merely means that the affected substance abuser will think in ways that are extremely irrational (i.e., often justify the substance abuse, rationalizing the abuse, minimizing abuse or harmful behaviors, constantly comparing, blaming situations and others, and feeling victimized). It is these denial mechanisms I referred to as the "fortress of denial" that allows the user to continue to use and avoid the painful consequences and feelings of their continued addiction. Therefore, one of the first aspects of substance abuse counseling is addressing some of these denial mechanisms and irrational beliefs that perpetuate continued use. In some case it takes a long time of emotional pain to abandon the reservations that avoid a commitment to abstinence. The most common reservations is the irrational belief "I can use differently, or control my use one more time". Oddly, the outcome is the same: more hardship and deeper negative consequences.

The Social Component of addiction:

Addiction eventually erodes trust, intimacy, and respect from all relationships. The damage to relationships can literally rip a family system apart. The family and relational damage is nothing short of heart breaking, often the damage is so severe that reconciliation and repair can take a life time. Observationally, I have noticed that the younger a person starts using drugs the more injured they are in the area of attachment. In fact, many long time users will find it utterly painful to merely "be" and "relate" with others. The reason is simple- while most children and teens are learning how to engage and maintain relations; users were preoccupied with using and or recovering from using, so they stopped growing in this vital aspect of life; Hence, when many substance abusers "hit bottom": many users have virtually no relational resources because of the tendency to withdraw and isolate. The damage in this area seems to be driven by shame, social anxiety and a painful awkwardness that can last a life- time. Relational counseling is vital in early recovery as well as a 12 step program or a faith community which facilitates inter-personal relationships. The disease of addiction is unfortunately marked by deception, manipulation, and a selfishness that will destroy even the most loving relationships. As one pursues getting high nothing really matters so many relationships are destroyed or damaged long before a substance abuser "hits bottom" or finds treatment and early stabilization. The element of shame and profound regret often hinders reconciliation until deep amends and forgiveness is established.

The Spiritual Component of addiction:

Contrary to many, this author truly feels there is a strong spiritual component to addiction. The premise is derived from the text of AA and years of antidotal experiences that seem to confirm this aspect of addiction. "The Big Book of AA" maintains "resentment is the number one offender. It destroys more alcoholics than anything else: From it stems all forms of spiritual disease, for we have been not only mentally and physically ill, we have been *spiritually sick*- When the spiritual malady is overcome, we straighten out mentally and physically". Moreover, the disease of addiction tends to rob one from a "conscious contact with The God of one's understanding" This lack of spirituality tends to contribute to a lack of hope.

The tendency to drift away is due to the attachment to the drug and the shame that follow the addict long into recovery. Like Adam and Eve, the addict often runs and hides because of the attachment to the drug and the shame that comes from being an addict/alcoholic. He or she may continue to "run and withdraw" until they can't do so anymore. Shame is a very pervasive factor in addiction.

Eventually, an addict or alcoholic will eventually reach a state of utter exhaustion; a "place "that is characterized by burning out all their relational resources, and placed in such misery that they are finally constrained to surrender their will to the God of their understanding, or continue to "use themselves to death". It is at this point, the addict or alcoholic gets "real" and a moment of clarity finally beacons. It is only at this point "one may see the Face of God" At this stage of helplessness one becomes coachable and able to "do whatever it takes to stay clean and sober". Until one reaches this point of surrender, entering into recovery is often improbable. Many clinicians feel they can "bring the bottom to the addict" and this will be enough for the addict to cease the addiction, but this is seldom the case. Although, this type of intervention is often inept, it should be employed to try and save lives and diminish the use. Miracles do happen!

WHAT IS RECOVERY?

I have always maintained that good recovery from any addiction is reflected in balance and a general feeling of internal and external wellness. Because of this rather vague yet elegant definition let me extrapolate on the importance of balance, and what I mean by "the feeling of wellness". Balance refers to a sense of equilibrium and stability in the same four areas that addiction affects. These areas have been discussed in the previous article on *The Components of Addiction*. It is clear, stable and thriving recovery is a life dedicated to maintaining some balance in the following critical areas:

1. The neurobiological realm: (brain functioning)

I earnestly, believe that when co-occurring mental illness is not treated one's recovery is greatly diminished to "white knuckling" it through life and eventual relapse. A recovery that is marked by abstinence based symptoms (i.e., debilitating social anxiety, depression and mood disorders) is nothing short of torture. Because of attitudinal barriers to access mental health I have seen many suffer, alienate themselves, and eventually relapse. Gaining stability and addressing one's mental illness is a huge part in one's recovery and should never be ignored. Over the years I have seen so many miracles and lives changed because they were effectively treated with psychotropic medications.

2. The psychological realm:

When one addresses "the stinking thinking" and addresses the many denial mechanisms (i.e., denial, inability to embrace responsibility, minimizing, rationalizing, blaming, feeling like a victim, and justifying) and starts to live life on life's terms one will began to grow. For the user the ability to move away from the denial mechanisms is critical for progress. Growth in this area is extremely arduous and if one doesn't have courage and "a reason to win", growth will be stunted: Hence, long term therapy and or substance abuse counseling is highly recommended to aid in maintaining balance and avoiding relapses of all kinds. It should be said, the therapeutic importance of continued therapy does not stop with "double digit" years in recovery.

3. The social realm:

In this area the recovering person is committed to work on social skills that allow them to maintain healthy replicating relationships that are meaningful. This is also a huge piece in recovery. If manipulation and dishonesty is still paramount, this area of one's life will suffer greatly. If the recovering individual never acquires the social skills "to be and relate" they will sadly resort to isolation. The tendency to isolate and withdraw is always a concern for recovering folks because one needs relational resources and relationships to grow. Often if one area is lacking there may be serious ramifications such as relapse, interpersonal conflict, and maladaptive patterns of coping due to chronic stress.

Frequently, one's ability to handle stress effectively declines due to a lack of balance in the four identified areas. Often, fatigue sets in and compromises insight and judgment. When growth is constrained in this area of one's recovery, it is usually met with deep insecurities, tears, and increased abstinence based symptoms that almost always guarantees relapse.

A special note on individuals who have started drug use early in their adolescence: their primary challenge will be in this area because they merely never adequately learned how to "be" and "relate" with others in a healthy manner. This ineptness in the inter-personal realm is due to the preoccupation with getting high during a pivotal time of brain development. State dependent learning was at play, meaning they learned how to do relationship high! Their primary attachment was to the drugs or alcohol; therefore, this social piece in their recovery will plague many, well into the double digit years of recovery. The goal in this realm is to learn to contribute to others to a cause that is "greater than one's self". Most individuals in the field seem to forget that recovery is relationally driven and relationships are paramount for growth.

4. The spiritual realm:

Over the course of 25 years of counseling substance abusers, I have realized no alcoholic, addict, or any other person with a process addiction ever finds recovery without an existential purpose to get clean! I call this vital motivation, "a reason to win". Without an existential purpose (a hope) a person will be driven to continue to use in spite of painful circumstances. It is heart wrenching to see the disease ravish the human body, mind and spirit of a human being because hope which has been abandoned. Therefore, good recovery finds an existential reason to stay clean. In the development of this aspect of recovery one may explore religion. Often, religion plays a huge role in one's conversion/recovery, and sparks deeper spirituality that transcends any type of organized religion. In the rooms of AA, it is a "conscious contact with one's higher power" that facilitates a reason bigger then oneself to go through the pain of recovery and sustain abstinence. Moreover, I believe that when one is using, they lose their conscious contact with their Creator and as a result loses the "relational ability" that can provide strength and solace. Thus, many emerge into a spiritual malaise (remember the attachment aspect of addiction and the hi-jacked brain principle) which fuels the "self will run riot" facet of addiction. This self-will is manifested by irrational beliefs and a sense of hubris that validates the notion that "I have it together, I can use on my own terms; I got this under control, and somehow consequences will not impact me because I am an exception". In some rare cases, all hope is sadly abandoned and the addict or alcoholic commits himself/herself entirely to staying high until they are institutionalized, arrested, or they expire.

Extraordinarily, over the years I have noticed that it is the "hope to die cases" that appear to find recovery in a more secure manner, and they end up thriving in their recovery! It is these difficulty populations that seem to "get it" because when they are ready to change-they truly change! In this unique population, there is almost always a huge cataclysmic spiritual conversion that anchors "the reason to win". It is both fascinating and mind blowing to see this change transform in a person's life. I think when one is still deceived into believing they have yet another recovery opportunity to pursue, "so they might as well continue to use". This is nothing short of a life threatening reservations about recovery. As a result, they "run on self-will", and operate under the fallacy that they are in control of their use. It is this denial that fuels the belief that consequences of their use will somehow bypass them because they are "uniquely special" As a clinician, my primary role is to provide hope so an individual can transcend and try to penetrate the wall of denial. Readiness for change is the sacred spot I covet for all still struggling with addiction. Unfortunately, many addicts only get to this place by intense pain which always seems to be an effective task master in comparison to "bringing the bottom to an addict".

Characteristics of Healthy Recovery

I earnestly believe recovery from most diseases and or substance abuse must embrace balance in the following five dimensions: Below are five marks of healthy recovery that seem to be the hallmarks of the primary goal for all in recovery- maintenance recovery!

- Physical and Psychological Wellbeing: One generally feels somewhat comfortable in their skin, and any discomfort is tolerable. One has learned the art of balance and the coping skills needed to manage one's disease(s). They are living in a healthy manner practicing self-care.

- A Sound safe Housing that support recovery: a stable and safe place to live and call home: A place that supports recovery and a life style of being clean and sober.

- Experiencing a sense of Community: learning how to sustain relationships and social networks that provide support, friendship, love, and nurture a sense of purpose. This community connection will always entail healthy accountability and clear boundaries

- "Embracing A reason to win:": Obtaining and sustaining a sense of purpose and spiritual significance by engaging in meaningful daily activities, such as a job, school, volunteerism, family caretaking, or creative endeavors, and achieving some autonomy to contribute to others in a meaningful manner

A Brief Word about Relapse

I earnestly believe that most relapses are a result of an accumulation of three specific situations which take place simultaneously and eventually result in a relapse:

- **The loss of a balance in recovery:** The loss of balance simply means, one begins to lose sight of the importance of managing all the core facets of recovery in a manner that sustains homeostasis. For example, working too much and forgetting to address mental health issues (i.e., anxiety or depression) or decreasing attendance of church or their home meetings. A couple of popular examples include the following: "I am eliminating therapy due to "feeling better" because I am attending church, or "my 12 step sponsor does not want me to continue taking my meds"

- **A break down in coping skills to effectively manage stress:** Many individuals in recovery fail to stop and ask for help when they "hit a wall" in their recovery so they began to revert back to old coping skills that are unhealthy and maladaptive in nature. This break down in healthy ways to cope begins to set the stage for anadonia, fatigue, and chronic distress. As a result, many do what is deemed "most reasonable" they self-medicate to alleviate the knowing discomfort

- **An erosion of central beliefs about recovery and subtle reservations:** Unfortunately, recovery takes vigilance, accountability and a firm commitment to growth. Should reservations about recovery creep back in and foster high risk behaviors relapse is imminent. Reservations are faulty beliefs about drug use (i.e., "I can drink one or two, it won't hurt me", "I can use pot after all it is natural", or "I am healed I don't need meetings or church anymore", or "I just don't need accountability"). All of these fallacies create a barrier to sustained recovery and give way to justifying drug use.

When one experiences all three situations at once for a sustained period of time relapse is almost guaranteed and often many don't make it back. Personal maintenance and spirituality of one's recovery is often a life or death situation. As The Big Book of Alcoholics Anonymous conveys so eloquently this gravity: "What we really have is a daily reprieve contingent on the maintenance of our spiritual program"- Page 85.

DAY 1

Seek to Understand Suffering...

Isaiah 58:4-6

Yesterday was Good Friday. In remembrance of Christ, my family and I had the opportunity to once again attend a "Tenebrae" service which was very meaningful. Please allow me to tell you a little about its history of it. For centuries, believers gathered as the sun set on Good Friday. (Whether the passion of Christ actually fell on a Friday was not what mattered but the significance of what occurred was the emphasis). Believers gathered to recall those hours of darkness that covered the world at the crucifixion of Jesus Christ. This worship service, called Tenebrae ('ten eh bray) from the Latin word for darkness, was a time of quiet reflection. It began at sunset, literally as the day turned into darkness. The scripture says LIGHT came into the world in the person of Jesus Christ, only to be rejected, scourged and crucified. The tradition was that the service would end as the final moments of the cross were remembered. In silence, the worshippers would leave the church building, without saying a word until they returned home. It occurred to me that maybe someone had not heard of Jesus or what he was sent here to do.

The reality is that His suffering was something we could not bear ourselves. Have you ever read what Isaiah prophesied in Isaiah chapter 53:4-6? He spoke clearly of God's plan for the suffering of the coming Messiah: "Surely he has borne our griefs and carried our sorrows; yet we esteemed him stricken, smitten by God, and afflicted. But he was wounded for our transgressions; he was crushed for our iniquities; upon him was the chastisement that brought us peace, and with his stripes (scourging) we are healed. All we like sheep have gone astray; we have turned---every one---to his own way; and the Lord has laid ON HIM (JESUS) the iniquity of us all".

Prayer for today: May I be mindful today that In Him (Jesus) was life, and the life was the light of men-and the light shines in darkness, and the darkness does not comprehend it. (John 1:4-5)

Action Today: Be a light wherever your station in life may be today. Concentrate on providing kindness and solutions to those around you

DAY 2

What is Your Deep Metaphor? Don't be fooled!

Mt.17:1-2

The deep metaphor to Individual Psychology is definitely a symbol (metaphor) that represents the epitome of healthy personal growth, or more specifically, "The Perfection of Humankind for a Utopia" (Adler, 1979). Nevertheless, the perfection aspect can be rather ambiguous, so to be more descriptive, the term that personal psychological growth encapsulates is the process of becoming healthy, and well adjusted: for the attainment of healthy and improved social adjustments. According to most theoretical positions, the aim and connotations at their core is the process of human excellence… This is essentially what psychology endeavors to achieve. Alfred Adler, the founder of Individual psychology called this the science of living, a concept which stems from a preoccupation with social interest and an attaining growth through one's own intuitive abilities: Hence, humanism's core tenets will ultimately place personal growth (a form of self-actualization) as the answer to one's psychological maladies. The goal of this ideology is to stimulate one to "reach beyond ourselves or self-imposed limits and encourages us to meet life's challenges with courage and cooperation, so that we express social interest in all we do" (Drescher & Stone 2004). Unbridled personal development is not our aim.

On the other hand, the Christian's metaphor is a radical one, a metaphor of transformation which entails God's sweet grace, mercy and redemptive power! For example, the word "transformed"…Comes from the Greek word metamorphoo {met-am-or-fo'-o} which means "to change into another form, to transform-, to transfigure". When in relationship with God this is happening automatically as we position ourselves to be transformed by His word, and the use of others in fellowship with one another! This word is powerful. Again, "metamorphosis" is derived from this word, which we use to describe the process of a caterpillar changing into a butterfly. One of the best usages of the word is utilized to describe Jesus on the Mount of Transfiguration! (Mt.17:1-2). Wow! See the metaphor- the symbol of our life is so radical, it embraces this transformation process. This is why Paul proclaimed to others relying on their own abilities to change in the following manner: "I have been crucified with Christ; and it is no longer who lives, but Christ living in me: and that life which I now live in the flesh I live by faith, the faith which is in the Son of God, who loved me, and gave himself up for me (Galatians 2:20)

Prayer for today: Heavenly Father reveal a healthy metaphor (a clear and healthy image) for my life and give me the strength to "*hold fast to your unchanging hand*"

Action for today: I will trust God today for my development by praising him for my growth regardless of how I feel or what is going on in my life.

DAY 3

Focus and Commit… Jesus is The Solution to all your Woes

Hebrews 3:1-6

"Therefore, holy brothers and sisters, who share in the heavenly calling, fix your thoughts on Jesus, whom we acknowledge as our apostle and high priest. He was faithful to the one who appointed him, just as Moses was faithful in all God's house. Jesus has been found worthy of greater honor than Moses, just as the builder of a house has greater honor than the house itself: For every house is built by someone, but God is the builder of everything. "Moses was faithful as a servant in all God's house, [a] bearing witness to what would be spoken by God in the future. But Christ is faithful as the Son over God's house. And we are his house, if indeed we hold firmly to our confidence and the hope in which we glory". Heb 3:1-6

Prayer for today: "My Creator (Lord), I am now willing that you should have all of me, good and bad. I pray that you now remove from me every single defect of character which stands in the way of my usefulness to you and my fellows. Grant me strength, as I go from here, to do your bidding". Amen." The Step Seven Prayer: The 12 steps for Alcoholics Anonymous Page76

Action for today: Focus today on helping another and being an encouragement.

DAY 4

"Consequently, he is able to save to the uttermost those who draw near to God through him, since he always lives to make intercession for them".

Hebrews 7:25

(A short excerpt from the personal journal of Eddie Olivas 7 days after brain surgery)

Over the last few weeks this writer has been plunged into a world of intense and relentless physical suffering: a pain that has eventually curtailed to a somewhat manageable level. The pain at one point swaddled me with its relentless and insurmountable migraines…The entire experience dinned into my mind many lessons on the God's perspective of suffering and my relationship with the Lord. After many years of suffering from a neurological condition called Trigeminal Neuralgia (a severe neurological disorder characterized by face pain on the left side of one's face, phantom toothaches, and intense migraines) I was constrained to make a decision: surgery or pain…

I was highly motivated to find a solution to my problem that would be both effective and not include a whole gaggle of narcotics. I believed the solution would be Micro Vascular Decompression Surgery, which I decided to undergo. The surgery went well: they separated the Trigeminal Nerve from an offending artery (a vascular loop); however, recovery continues to be filled with massive debilitating headaches, (air bubbles in the head, don't laugh) unyielding nausea and intense pain that radiates from my 5 inch incision at the base of my skull and travels down to the base of my tail bone. For seven days this pain wracked my body, I was feeling helpless, and upset that perhaps there was a possibility that maybe I made a terrible mistake… I remember, one particular day (day three) which was very hard: it entailed vomiting, intense pain, and two seizures, when I realized the condition was progressive and I could not pray, I cried out "Lord please help me, have mercy upon my soul". My wife said I repeated this over and over. It was at this point, I remember taking a slight turn for the better when a Doctor suddenly came into my room and made several different med orders and reassured me that "this would pass". I was experiencing severe effects from anesthesia which included extreme fatigue, stomach pain, back and leg pain and severe headaches, all of which was coupled with a swollen cerebellum which triggered the seizures.

In life, there will be intense pain that rocks one's cortical ability to transcend to a place in one's mind where one can file and restructure a reason for intense suffering. In my case, relief only came from crying out to my heavenly Father who heard my cries, and the prayers of good people that have been worthy to be called friends. Today, I am on a slow mend and progressing daily.

Prayer for today: Lord help me realize just a glimpse of your love for me today and focus my mind on your sweet forgiving grace through Christ Jesus

Action for today: May I demonstrate kindness and grace to someone who is suffering today.

DAY 5

"Enter into His Refuge…"

Psalms 91:1-4

"Whoever dwells in the shelter of the Most High will rest in the shadow of the Almighty, I will say of the Lord, "He is my refuge and my fortress my God, in whom I trust. Surely he will save you from the fowler's snare and from the deadly pestilence. He will cover you with his feathers, and under his wings you will find refuge" (Psalms 91 1-4)

Whatever, you may be struggling with, hold on and turn your attention to the Lord for He is the answer to your dilemma and the Peace for your weary soul…

Prayer for today: Lord help me today to enter into your refuge, help me concentrate on your protection and the gentle care that you bestow upon me.

Action for today: Make a concerted effort to meditate on the wonderful image of God's fortress and abandon a care that has thwarted you from being at peace.

DAY 6

"I do not write these things to make you ashamed, but to admonish you as my beloved children. For though you have countless guides in Christ, you do not have many fathers"

(1 Corinthians 4:14-16)

The Apostle Paul was most insightful in his thought about the significant difference between "guides and Fathers". Although Father's day has passed, let us be mindful of the importance of Fathers in both our personal lives and in our society. In a day and age where Fatherhood has fallen on hard times, let us be mindful to pray for courage and insight for the men in our lives that are Fathers as well as those who have stepped in to fill the void.

The Greek word for Father implies both the giver of life and "being committed to it" (Gk: patⴰr – father; one who imparts life and is committed to it; a progenitor, bringing into being to pass on the potential for likeness). In modern day Fatherhood, it appears that the commitment piece is lacking. One significant culprit for this break down is a lack of accountability and training: Hence, this week I implore you to pray for the Fathers in your life, that they may be able to rise up and face the responsibilities of their roles with commitment and love.

Prayer for today: Lord help me develop the courage and sensitivity to improve my relationship with my father, or a mentor I look up to.

Action for today: Bless your father with a visit or a phone call today. If there is pain or resentment, please ask the Lord to heal you so you can move on in your spirituality without the "barnacles of pain" from your family of origin. If you do not have a father perhaps, you can express your gratitude to a mentor who has been instrumental in your development.

DAY 7

"Love is patient, love is kind. It does not envy, it does not boast, it is not proud. It does not dishonor others, it is not self-seeking, it is not easily angered, and it keeps no record of wrongs. Love does not delight in evil but rejoices with the truth. It always protects, always trusts, always hopes, always perseveres"

1 Corinthians 13:4-7

Are you having inter-personal problems, and conflict? Go back to the basics on love….Dig deep within and pray that God imparts to you the power to love, forgive, and transcend to place where we seek God's approval….

In life, there will be major inter-personal conflicts and difficulties. As many are aware, we are truly powerless over what others think or how they may behave: however, we do have power to love with unconditional positive regard. My prayer is that we all come to realize the Love of God that will allow us to love the ugly, the disrespectful and the insensitive….

Prayer for today: Lord please help me to be more loving, especially to individuals who are "unlovable" in my life.

Action today: I will demonstrate the love of God to someone in my life that may be difficult or challenging

DAY 8

"Here I am". The affirmative response from Abraham…

Genesis 22:1.

The Hebrew expression *Hineni* (Here I am) which is found in the New Testament truly denotes to an eagerness to please. Hineni is explained most eloquently in the wonderful book "Life Lessons from the Monastery", by Jerome Kodel. Hineni is the Hebrew word which signifies a response of eagerness to obey -"Here I am" from a human standpoint, was used when Abraham in preparation of sacrificing Isaac, responded to God by saying Hineni (Genesis 22:1). He was actually ready to sacrifice his son in obedience to God when he responded to God by saying Hineni! (Here I am). When we see Isaiah answer the call of God we again see Hineni being applied (Isaiah 58:9). Here I am essentially means; I am here for you my Lord, my God, and Maker. The word conveys obedience, willingness, surrender, and perhaps an eagerness to please.

Regrettably, like most believers we were often short on saying Hineni; As a result, God was not short on responding by saying Hineni to both Abraham and Isaiah! When you find yourself slammed by both economic challenges and deep personal tests which constrained you to cry out, Oh Lord, please help me! His response to your cries will be nothing short of Hineni-HERE I AM. There is no doubt we serve a loving God that is gracious, kind, and faithful! During your darkest hours when you have lost all hope God will still be there- He is truly Emanuel, ready to say Hineni!

Prayer for today: Dear lord, help me say yes "here I am" to you. Help me abandon my stubborn will in areas of my life where I have been obstinate

Action today: Create a space in your environment where you can spend a moment with The Lord and reflect upon areas in your life that need surrender

Day 9

A Living Sacrifice..."Therefore, I urge you, brothers and sisters, in view of God's mercy, to offer your bodies as a living sacrifice, holy and pleasing to God—this is your true and proper worship. Do not conform to the pattern of this world, but be transformed by the renewing of your mind. Then you will be able to test and approve what God's will is—his good, pleasing and perfect will".

(Romans 12:1-2)

Prayer for today:

"God, I offer myself to thee - to build with me and do with me as Thou wilt. Relieve me of the bondage of self, that I may better do Thy will. Take away my difficulties, that victory over them may bear witness to those I would help of Thy Power, Thy Love and Thy Way of life. May I do Thy will always" **(63:2 original manuscript; 3rd Step Prayer from "The Big Book of AA)**

Action for today: Surrender to The lord and let go and let God...for he will give you peace for your weary mind.

DAY 10

"Seek first his kingdom and his righteousness, and all these things will be given to you as well"

(Mathew 6:33)

Having the unique opportunity to work as a therapist at an acute psychiatric hospital, I see many individuals because of both mental decomposition and, sudden unforeseen crisis that outweigh one's ability to deal with crushing circumstances. Over the years, I have facilitated thousands of groups and heard many stories. Recently, I heard one gentleman lament about putting God first. His lamentation seemed to oddly displace the pain and sorrow of his peers and penetrate the depths of our souls. His spring loaded message seemed out of place at first, and then it began to resonate and nurture the parched souls in our company. I remember the event vividly, for the message burned into my soul- a message of life. The middle age man, (who resembled Jack Nicholson in the "The Shinning") stood up, slightly stooped and proclaimed: "The Bible says Seek first his kingdom and his righteousness, and all these things will be given to you as well, I put God in the 3rd slot. I put my friends and my job first, then my wife and family second. Oddly God still blessed my household, but just think how much he would have done if I put him first! Do you think he doesn't have my attention now? You better believe he does!"

The essence of what was being communicated is the importance of placing God in "the first slot" so we will not live a life of regrets. Also, the message carried with it a warning: don't be fooled by putting your job and family before God because it makes sense...

Prayer for today: Lord allow me to be steadfast in putting you first in all that I do, especially in the area of interacting with others. May I live my life for an audience of one: thee, my heavenly Father!

Action for today: I will endeavor to evaluate my priorities and put God first in my life that He may have preeminence in all aspects of my life

DAY 11

And Don't Forget the House of Caesar…

"Greet all the saints in Christ Jesus. The brothers who are with me send greetings. All the saints send you greetings, especially those who belong to Caesar's household".

Philippians 4:21-22

One of the most opposing systems and emperors to The Christian faith was that of the Roman Empire. At the height of its reign Caesar perpetuated a climate that was extremely anti God. Nevertheless, in spite of this adversarial culture many Roman citizens were converted to Christianity. In the life of Paul we see God use him in a dramatic way, even at his lowest crisis in jail with Roman guards..

When Paul was at his lowest point in his life he made a decision to transcend and embrace a higher purpose. For Paul, it appeared prison would be his final destiny, yet he chose to have an impact in the lives of the Roman soldiers to such a degree that he communicates to the Philippians to send his greetings "especially to Caesars's Household". Wow!

Could you imagine being chained to a brutish Roman soldier for extended periods of time? Paul used the opportunity to mentor, teach and eventually communicate the truth of The Gospel of Christ which liberated both Paul and the many soldiers of the House of Caesar.

What is God doing in my Life and how should I respond?

My friend, you may be in paralyzing crisis in your life-a complete stand still with all options exhausted. Don't give up! By faith you too can be liberated and be used of God to do some very impactful work for God's kingdom. It is very clear that when we are in the valley of darkness God does his best work. I love his grace and mercy in that it drives us to our knees in obedience and sweet adoration!

Prayer for today: Lord I pray for guidance today, help me come to understand your purpose in my life. I avail myself to thee

Action for today: I will endeavor to evaluate my life and determine to answer the paramount question: "What is God doing in my life and how should I respond?"

DAY 12

"Only be careful, and watch yourselves closely so that you do not forget the things your eyes have seen or let them slip from your heart as long as you live. Teach them to your children and to their children after them".

Deuteronomy 4:9

The slightly sedated middle age women experiencing a medical detox after many years of alcoholism conveyed to her peers while in a therapeutic group: " I use to say when I get older I'm never going to set forth in a Church ever again". Working as a therapist in many different milieus of treatment gives me a window into the soul of hurting humanity. I remember recently, a process group where a woman was lamenting: "When I was a child I was dragged to church every time the doors were open, (this is a familiar story with many of our youth) and now that I have ruined my life, I realize Christ is still with me every step of the way and his grace is sufficient for my recovery.

This is an unfortunate reoccurring story for many in the Church and the redundancy of the story truly "chaffs my behind". At times there seems to be so many of the Church's children ending up living irresponsible, reckless lives that bring forth sorrow. I hear this story several times a year: the story of a Church youth who later falls away as an adult. Often this rebellion is a direct result of forced church attendance and a rigid theology. Unfortunately, many of the churches' wounded find themselves living a life of self-destruction until "coming to their senses".

As a parent of two teens, I see the importance of living out my Christianity on a daily basis rather than emphasizing a stern approach to rigid church attendance void of parental teaching, forming, and emulating. I want to communicate through orthodoxy and orthopraxy, a lifestyle that reflects the presence of Jesus and what it means to be a follower of "The Way"… This means I strive to teach my children "the ways of God" and a respectful attitude towards the purpose of the church. The ultimate goal of our parenting is to KNOW Christ and the knowledge of his power. God bless all of our kids

Prayer for today: Lord help me be mindful of ways I can be a better example to those around me, and a better parent to my children

Action for today: May I encourage my children today and examine my convictions to ensure they match up with my behavior. Help me show them unconditional positive regards without conditions.

DAY 13

Leadership: Transferring Knowledge and Direction to the next Generation...

"Now Elisha was fallen sick of his sickness whereof he died. And Joash the king of Israel came down unto him, and wept over his face, and said, O my father, my father, the chariot of Israel, and the horsemen thereof. And Elisha said unto him, take bow and arrows. And he took unto him bow and arrows. And he said to the king of Israel; Put thine hand upon the bow. And he put his hand upon it: and Elisha put his hands upon the king's hands. And he said, Open the window eastward. And he opened it. Then Elisha said, Shoot. And he shot. And he said, the arrow of the LORD'S deliverance, and the arrow of deliverance from Syria: for thou shalt smite the Syrians in Aphek, till thou have consumed them"

2nd Kings 13:14-20)

This is a wonderful story that communicates the essence of leadership and the value of applied wisdom as it is transferred to younger generations: My prayer is that we all come to realize the value of this interchange between those who have the experience and sage to win battles and those who are fervent, however, less skilled. Often what is learned is experientially internalized by such simple acts as offering a little direction and emotional support. The outcomes can bring forth victories beyond our expectations.

Prayer for today: I pray today that I may understand the importance of legacy that transcends to deeper meaning of the mundane-May I come to know God's purpose in my life as it relates to leaving a "divine legacy life eternal".

Action today: I will be proactive in looking at what I can plan, lead, organize and control in my life. What I cannot control in my life I will defer to God.

DAY 14

He Has Risen!

"Therefore he is able also to save them to the uttermost that comes unto God by him, seeing he ever lives to make intercession for them". Amen!

Hebrews 7:25

The hurried churchman was marveling at the attendance of the recent Sunday service and the many new converts who were drawn to church during this wonderful time of year. It was a busy time for parish/church life and it was easy for him to lose his focus of what Easter really represented until he realized his error.

May Easter be remembered every day and may we be mindful of Christ and contemplate the significance of the work on Calvary: Let us spend time in thoughtful prayer and focus on Christ: His death, Burial, and Glorious Resurrection. May this perspective bring comfort to you for any anxiety or worry you may be enduring at this time.

Prayer for today: Lord I thank you for saving me and giving me eternal life. I will be glad and rejoice in spite of whatever I am going through!

Action for today: I will express my gratitude about God's love to someone I know today.

DAY 15

"Now faith is the substance of things hoped for, the evidence of things not seen".

Hebrews 11:1

What is Faith and why is it so essential for meaningful growth? Faith in a Judeo Christian perspective is critical to a believer's growth and an eternal perspective. To individuals who do not share similar views it is merely another point of view. For a Christian one's faith traditions and beliefs deserve constant evaluation. This particular acknowledgement of one's faith aids greatly in the process of integrating one's psychology with one's theology.

Hence, if you are going through a season in your life where you are questioning your faith, and having difficulty integrating your world view with your core convictions, pray to God and seek discernment in your time of darkness for He will give you the faith needed to help with the "evidence not seen".

Prayer for today: Heavenly Father please give me faith to trust in you and your word. Allow me the courage "to reach through the clouds of doubt and grab a hold of God's word".

Action for today: Today I will remind myself and verbalize "God loves me; I am a child of God, and I can trust Him concerning my situation.

DAY 16

"Whoever dwells in the shelter of the Most High will rest in the shadow of the Almighty. I will say of the Lord, "He is my refuge and my fortress my God, in whom I trust." Surely He (God) will save you from the fowler's snare and from the deadly pestilence. He will cover you with his feathers, and under his wings you will find refuge"

Psalms 91: 1-4

Whatever, you may be struggling with today, hold on and turn your attention to The Lord for He is the answer to your dilemma and the peace for your weary soul...

Prayer for today: Dear Lord, I am weary and have many concerns, Please give me grace to endure my situation.

Action for today: Today I will release my concern and be kind to myself by resting for a moment: During this time I will concentrate and dwell under the umbrella of God's grace.

DAY 17

Returning to the basics of Love: "Love is patient, love is kind. It does not envy, it does not boast, it is not proud. It does not dishonor others, it is not self-seeking, it is not easily angered, it keeps no record of wrongs. Love does not delight in evil but rejoices with the truth. It always protects, always trusts, always hopes, always perseveres"

1 Cor13:4-7

Are you having interpersonal problems, and conflict? Go back to the basics and love....Dig deep within and pray that God imparts to you the power to love, forgive, and transcend to a place where we seek God's approval....

In life, there will be major inter-personal conflicts and difficulties. As many are aware, we are truly powerless over what others think or how they may behave: however, what we do have is the power to love with unconditional positive regard. My prayer is that we all come to realize the Love of God which allows us to love the ugly, the disrespectful and insensitive....

Prayer for today: Heavily Father, I have many character defects that have been a detriment in so many ways- Please help me overcome my defects and surrender them to you

Action for today: I will take a moment and write down my besetting character defects and share them with someone who may be able to encourage and pray for me.

DAY 18

"My old self has been crucified with Christ. It is no longer I who live, but Christ who lives in me: So I live in this earthly body by trusting in the Son of God, who loved me and gave himself for me."

Galatians 2:20

The Apostle Paul wrote many truths. One of the more remarkable points was to the Galatians. How often do we forget such riveting and simplistic lessons? For example, one new Christian shared a recent story that solidifies my point: "I prepared my heart in prayer and meditation for the big Easter service. I had to try to reel in my anticipation for a heavy intellectual argument proving the Resurrection of Christ Jesus. I was ready for a great, intellectually; engaging message (i.e., apologetics, and other Resurrection positions) yet what I heard was extremely simple. Incidentally, what he experienced was completely different from what he was ready for. That Easter morning was nothing short of powerful and stirring, a message that made him marvel….The message was nothing short of cataclysmic in that The Word of God burned into his soul a hope that transformed him forever! The message was elegant and simple, eternal hope for those who believe in Jesus Christ

It is in these encounters (simple communications) we find the evidence of the power of God. Often we are like my new convert friend and forget that the biggest evidence of the Resurrection is you and me and the stirring simple account of the Resurrection of Jesus Christ

Prayer for today: Today is my day of salvation. You Lord, are my Lord and my Savior from sin, sickness and eternal death. Make the simplicity of this truth a reality in every facet of my life today.

Action for today: I will make a decision to recommit myself to God and invite his will to be done in all areas of my life.

DAY 19

Let Interruptions be Opportunities for the Love of God... "Let no one despise your youth, but be an example to the believers in word, in conduct, in love, in spirit, in faith, in purity."

1 TIM 4:12

As we began this new day let us all be mindful that throughout our busy day we will have many opportunities to express kindness and Grace to those who are suffering. Often, individuals will come into our sphere who are struggling with problems that our both painful and perplexing, they are in need of kindness and understanding. Our kindness and concern for them will speak volumes of love, and be an example to other Christians of how we should express our faith.

I remember on one specific occasion, a colleague of mine was recently "let go" and she was devastated. In an effort to extend grace to her my wife and I decided to invite her over for dinner. After a wonderful dinner, she started to cry...while holding her three year old she lamented "you don't even know what your kindness has meant to me, thank you so much". This situation with my colleague was burned into my soul of the power of kindness.

As Christians, try and find time to express kindness and grace to those whom God has put in your path, for it will truly speak volumes about God's love and grace. Very often we get preoccupied with our theology that we forget the insurmountable value of our demeanor.

Eddie Olivas III

Prayer for today: Dear Lord, fulfill my heart's desire to be a good example to my neighbors. May I express kindness and grace to those around me today

Action for today: I will "try to walk the extra mile for someone in need" and express kindness and grace to those whom God puts in my path

DAY 20

"You shall love the Lord your God with all your heart and with all your soul and with all your strength and with your entire mind, and your neighbor as yourself." Jesus

Luke 10:27

As a young man I often grappled with the existential (meaning) challenge of finding purpose for my life. It wasn't till recently, that I truly resolved this issue with internalized conviction. As believer's our purpose will more often than not be defined by our relationships with both our family and other believers in Christ; hence, our aim slightly changes as we traverse through the various seasons of our life.

Never the less, there is one purpose and role that never changes for us: To serve the Lord with all your heart, soul, strength, and thy neighbor as thy self! The great spiritual teacher Thomas Merton in his book, "No Man is an Island" provided a similar perspective that resonates with Jesus' teaching about devotion. Merton wrote: "When we have the right intention, our intention is pure. When we seek to do God's will with a super natural motive-we mean to please Him in all things".

Life is then condensed to one beautiful and elegant Pauline truth: "For in him we live, and move, and have our being", as certain also of your own poets who said "For we are also his offspring" Acts 17:28; therefore, our aim in life is simple: to please God by doing HIS will as we fulfill our various roles in life regardless of how mundane they may be...

Prayer for today: Lord, I commit my entire life to you. Remove any impure intentions that are displeasing to you.

Action for today: I will endeavor to meditate on the reality that I am your child, and that you love me. I can trust you in all situations

DAY 21

"Therefore, we are ambassadors for Christ, as though God were making an appeal through us; we beg you on behalf of Christ, be reconciled to God".2 Cor 5:20

2 Corinthians 5:20

A worried Chinese Father was burdened about his son departing to The United States: "Son do not forget who you are! My dear son, you're an ambassador and you're a reflection of your faith, family and our village". This statement resonates with the reality that we are truly Ambassadors, for Christ, or we our merely an envoy (representation) of self-interest for own agenda. Periodically, we all must ask the direct question: Who am I? May we all have the maturity to respond to this question with a resounding confirmation of God's hold on our lives and the reality that our lives matter in this world! We can in fact build community and reflect the love of God in our daily lives.

Pray for today: Dear Father, grant me the guidance for my life and reveal to me ways to be an effective Ambassador for Christ

Action for today: I will try and act as a representative of God and display his unconditional love.

DAY 22

"Dare Greatly and Challenge Yourself" (Exert from a Family Newsletter in 2008)

During this year, there were times when we had to simply bow our heads low and raise our hands high and cry out to the living God for help. We experienced valleys of weeping, and times of darkness which are always indicative of the "Hero's journey". We have realized, it is in these times in our lives (the uncomfortable times where situations seem dire) that we come face to face with the living God: in dark difficult times where we think we can't take another breath…and the next breath we do take is the breath of God!

In the Christian journey, it seems as if we need to get to this point to establish reliance on God. For this reason, it is now time to face 2014, and the most fitting outlook should be to look up! Face the year with optimism, faith, and a deep belief in the Utopia. This last year, I found that dreams, personal visions, and things that grip us to dare greatly have fallen on hard times…Hence, my challenge to all of us is to rest in the realm of the utopia-the unthinkable. I believe one person can make a huge difference in this world (i.e., the Nobel Peace Prize winner Norman Borlang, in 1970 was called "the man who fed the world") or, more practically, every day Hero's in your own life. I believe in creating communities for God. This entails creating loyalties through relationships, one person at a time. This slow arduous manner is the only effective way to promote the kingdom of God and facilitate the impossible!

I love the story of the feeding of the five thousand and Jesus' bristling question to Phillip. Phillip's response to his question provides a window into all of our souls, and captures the mind of most believers (believers who frequently think like their heathen counter parts), "Where shall we buy bread that these may eat" Jesus uttered (testing Phillip), for he himself knew what he would do. Of course, Philip answered Jesus with an earthly calculating response; "we have about 200 denarii's worth of bread…" (John 6:1-7) This response is in fact indicative of the natural mind. A mind that is unable to transcend and find spiritual significance and solutions to pressing everyday difficulties.

This coming year, strive to grow in the realm of the impossible, for in this realm you will find joy, meaning and purpose.

Pray for today: Lord please reveal to me your vision for my life and your purpose for me. I pray you "burn it into my heart like fire".

Action for today: I will take a moment and "listen to my heart"

DAY 23

"Then was Jesus led up of the Spirit into the wilderness to be tempted of the devil. And when he had fasted forty days and forty nights, he was afterward a hungred. And when the tempter came to him, he said, If thou be the Son of God, command that these stones be made bread: But he answered and said, It is written, Man shall not live by bread alone, but by every word that proceedeth out of the mouth of God. Then the devil taketh him up into the holy city, and setteth him on a pinnacle of the temple, And saith unto him, If thou be the Son of God, cast thyself down: for it is written, He shall give his angels charge concerning thee: and in their hands they shall bear thee up, lest at any time thou dash thy foot against a stone. Jesus said unto him, It is written again, Thou shalt not tempt the Lord thy God. Again, the devil taketh him up into an exceeding high mountain, and sheweth him all the kingdoms of the world, and the glory of them; And saith unto him, All these things will I give thee, if thou wilt fall down and worship me. Then saith Jesus unto him, Get thee hence, Satan: for it is written, Thou shalt worship the Lord thy God, and him only shalt thou serve. Then the devil leaveth him, and, behold, angels came and ministered unto him"

Matthew 4:1-11

As we start a new day, may we contemplate on this scriptural context, Jesus was confronted by the devil in three different ways that are very relevant to our spirituality: Firstly, Jesus's initial struggle was both about the "war of the flesh" and also with his identity, when the devil asked Jesus to display his power by "turning stone into bread". Jesus declined to "show off". Often, the world will try and define us by *what we do*. Thank God we are not what we do! Secondly, Jesus was challenged when the devil taunted him to demonstrate his ability to jump off the pinnacle to confirm what people of that day believed he could do. Unfortunately, dower results follow when we allow others to shape our identity. Thirdly, the devil tries yet again, to entice Jesus with an entire kingdom to try and persuade Jesus's purpose (i.e., become a worldly rich ruler of many possessions, and be successful). It is widely known that the world's influence is relentless in trying to define us and gain an edge on us by changing our purpose.

Prayer for today: God direct me, protect me, and reveal to me my core identity and show me ways that I can purposefully serve you better!

Action for today: I will be kind and gracious to myself today and forgive myself for any sins or mistakes that would interfere with our relationship

DAY 24

"And he will restore the hearts of the fathers to their children, and the hearts of the children to their fathers, lest I come and smite the land with a curse."

Malachi 4:6

"Just as a father has compassion on his children, so the LORD has compassion on those who fear Him".

Psalm 103:13

As a therapist working in the field of mental health and substance abuse treatment I have had the unique opportunity to counsel many men in various and diverse treatment settings. Often, men find themselves in treatment after long bouts of substance abuse or a behavioral addiction which has spiraled out of control. As a result of pain they are forced to seek out help, and sadly it is often too late. Over the years, I have noticed men in treatment have many variables in common: they find themselves alone, afraid, extremely angry, deeply ashamed, and/or suffered from a huge void which was left by an abusive or absentee Father. These feelings run rampant in almost all hurting men regardless of social economic strata, race, or their world view.

Moreover, often these men feel deeply marginalized and misunderstood in both their manhood and for seeking treatment for mental health issues that have adversely affected their lives. This pervasive feeling of marginalization seems to stem from a hazy sense of what a "man" should be like today, and an imprecise double standard that society has imposed upon men concerning both their identity and their role in society. Society in America places huge expectations on men without realizing in order to meet these expectations it is going to take both examples of healthy men and training from men who have been able to demonstrate success: Men who have been "equal to the task" are in fact becoming increasingly scant.

Prayer for today: Pray for all the men in your life. pray that God strengthen them and fulfill His destiny in their lives

Action for today: I will communicate my gratitude to a the men in my life who have "stayed the course"

DAY 25

"For My Grace is sufficient for you, for my power is made perfect in your weakness"- Jesus

(2Cor 12:9)

All our accomplishments are because of hard work and the Grace of God that has been bestowed upon you. Without Him they could not be achieved!

Pray for today: Meditate today on God's sweet Grace in your life, think upon God's Grace and enter into a deep attitude of gratitude: God's Grace is like a "kaleidoscope of many colors" Meditate on how God's Grace has been manifest in every aspect of your life.

Action for today: For today, I will trust actively in God's word: "His grace is sufficient" God is more than enough.

DAY 26

"Fear thou not; for I am with thee: be not dismayed; for I am thy God: I will strengthen thee; yea, I will help thee; yea, I will uphold thee with the right hand of my righteousness".

Isaiah 41:10

Periodically, I find myself fearful of situations in my life and my own inability to merely "BE". Often many individuals in recovery find it difficult to be content in their own skin. There are many reasons for this lack of personal acceptance. Due to past traumas, shame, and persistent fear many struggle. What is your struggle today? What do you fear or what are you trying to control today?

Take a moment to change your *focus* and your *state* and you will probably be able to change your perspective on perplexing perspectives: Focus on God's presence in your life and change your "position" as it relates to your situation (typically we want to detach). State and focus is a powerful coping skill when we surrender to God's word for God proclaims "fear thou not for I am with thee"

Prayer for today: Dear God, I cast my care upon you and embrace your presence in my life today. Help me *focus* on your love and presence, and allow me to change my *state* or my relationship to a problem in my life: Help me detach myself from my issues and perplexing situations

Action for today: I will cast my care unto the Lord and concentrate (*focus*) on God's presence in my life-I will try to be present for someone who is distraught or in need of some reassurance-this will help change my *state* as it relates to my need to get some space between myself and my issues.

DAY 27

"I pray also that the eyes of your heart may be enlightened in order that you may know the hope to which he has called you, the riches of his glorious inheritance in the saints, and his incomparably great power for us who believe. That power is like the working of his mighty strength, which he exerted in Christ when he raised him from the dead and seated him at his right hand in the heavenly realms, far above all rule and authority, power and dominion, and every title that can be given, not only in the present age but also in the one to come. And God placed all things under his feet and appointed him to be head over everything for the church, which is his body, the fullness of him who fills everything in every way".

Ephesians 1:18-23

As a devote Catholic growing up, I recall most in my neighborhood we went to church every Sunday. I remember getting up early to go to church and the importance of connecting with other of the same faith. This experience was distinct because it communicated the importance of God, faith, and community. Typically, every Sunday's most in my suburban community would go to Sunday Mass. The church experience was rich and very centering. The weekly ritual of attending Sunday Mass reiterated the importance of our relationship with God and it established a sense of closure of another week gone by. This ritual is embedded into my mind as a very pleasant noteworthy memory. Everything about going to our parish was meaningful from the smell of the incense to the religious symbols throughout the church. This religious ritual touched me in a uniquely spiritual way. Furthermore, the church was a place of refuge for my family and the faith community. As a young boy I could not cognitively articulate this sense of serenity, never the less, I was able to experience it with my senses…Today, I often seek refuge in church and I am able to "catch that feeling" of serenity and comfort. Church can be a very healing place, for those that are seeking truth, comfort and reassurance.

Pray for today: Intercede in prayer for your church that God may lead you to a church family where you can grow and contribute to others who can benefit from your experiences- A place where you can establish ritual and "calibrate your moral compass".

Action for today: Consider a church that may be for you.

DAY 28

Jesus conveyed: 'For this reason a man will leave his father and mother and be united to his wife, and the two will become one flesh'?

Mathew 19:5

In spite of the erosion of traditional marriage, I believe many marriages suffer unduly because of an inability to leave their parents or others to cleave to their wives…Successful marriages are often built upon a foundation of three: The man, his wife and most importantly Jesus. Thus, Gods promise is a three-fold cord CANNOT be broken. A marriage is not fully accomplished at the mere utterance of the vows or does this institution end after the honeymoon is over. A healthy marriage is a bond that is imitated and sustained by a commitment to God for this is referenced as "the great mystery" likened to the relationship between Christ and the Church" (Ephesians 5:30-32).

Prayer for today: Lord help me leave those things or individuals that compete with my need to "leave and cleave" to my wife.

Action for today: I will make a concerted effort to work on my marriage by putting my relationship with God first and encouraging my spouse to do the same. Also, I will work on improving intimacy by becoming more accessible emotionally.

DAY 29

"I beseech you therefore, brethren, by the mercies of God, that ye present your bodies a living sacrifice, holy, acceptable unto God, which is your reasonable service. And be not conformed to this world: but be ye transformed by the renewing of your mind, that ye may prove what is that good, and acceptable, and perfect, will of God. For I say, through the grace given unto me, to every man that is among you, not to think of himself more highly than he ought to think; but to think soberly, according as God hath dealt to every man the measure of faith".

Romans 12:1-3

Today is a new day for me to surrender and make an effort to conform my thoughts to God's word. I know the world's philosophy and often my thoughts are counter to God's word and his plan for my life: hence, the necessity to continue to transform my mind by renewing it with Gods healing word daily.

As those in recovery would say, "I need help with my stinking thinking"! Because of years of abuse or trauma we sometimes develop strange defense mechanisms that can thwart our spiritual development. Some of the more common "dysfunctional coping skills" are as followed: feeling like a victim with no power, projection, blaming, rationalizing and justifying. All of these beliefs and maladaptive behaviors which become part of denial can truly be counterproductive. Today, make an effort to renew your mind by dwelling on God's word and pray for strength to surrender totally to God, for He is the one who can grant you the ability to change in a unique and enduring way

Prayer for today: Lord God "Grant me the serenity to accept the things I cannot change; courage to change the things I can; and wisdom to know the difference. Enjoy one moment at a time; accepting hardships as the pathway to peace; (taking, as He did, this sinful world as it is), not as I would have it; trusting that He will make all things right if I surrender to His will; that I may be reasonably happy in this life and supremely happy with Him forever in the next. Amen". --Reinhold Niebuhr

Action for today: Write down on a piece of paper your number one dysfunctional coping skill, and commit it to God

DAY 30

In you, Lord my God, I put my trust. I trust in you; do not let me be put to shame, nor let my enemies triumph over me. No one who hopes in you will ever be put to shame but shame will come on those who are treacherous without cause. Show me your ways, Lord, teach me your paths.

Psalms 25:1-4

Today, I will earnestly try and stay in the moment and trust in God for all of my needs. Because of poor choices and addiction in the past, we have all been shamed with or without cause: however, today I know I will never be shamed because I will trust in God and his plan for my life.

Prayer for today: Dear Father, wash me and cleanse me from my past behaviors that were shameful. I know if I trust you and worship you I will be cleansed of the shame and guilt of my past

Action for today: I will bask in God's healing and forgiving love. I will make amends to myself and others for the damage I have done in the past. These amends may involve a special treat or providing self-care in the form of self-soothing behaviors for the self to calm and restore my sanity...

DAY 31

"I know your deeds, that you are neither cold nor hot. I wish you were either one or the other! So, because you are lukewarm - neither hot nor cold - I am about to spit you out of my mouth"

Revelations 3:15-16

There is only one reference in the Bible to a 'lukewarm' Christian and that is Revelation 3:15-16 which warns of the dangers of being "lukewarm". It is clear in scripture that God desires for us to love him with all our mind, body and soul. Nothing less will do. As one pioneer in Alcoholics Anonymous conveyed "I stopped playing with God when I had enough pain. Unfortunately, pain and discomfort is the only way I learn: Today, I can say half measures availed me nothing. Today, I am not half stepping in my spirituality or my recovery, and the results appear to be a peace of God that transcends all understanding".

Prayer for today: Lord, I am so tired of "half stepping" and being lukewarm, give me the strength to commit all that I am to you without reservations, for I know I will not be truly content until I give you my all in spite of my character defects.

Action for today: I will make a concerted effort to evaluate my spirituality and what I might need to aid in my spiritual growth (i. e., books, bible, bible helps and a quiet place to study). I am aware now, that my spiritual development and relationship with God is front and center in my life.

A word about Quality Recovery

When one looks at the benefits of a social support system, one can see the most evident: that being a part of a community aids in our overall health. In the rooms of a 12 step meeting one will find genuine acceptance and unconditional positive regard. These two characteristics are essential for growth and psychological healing. Moreover, being part of a supportive community allows for us to have a more quality recovery. Again, the principles of recovery are dependent on continued growth. A community that supports us will allow for us to have both accountability and allow us to develop in the following areas of recovery which have been laid out by SAMSHA (Substance Abuse and Mental Health Services Administration).

Guiding Principles of Recovery:

- Recovery emerges from hope: The belief that recovery is real provides the essential and motivating message of a better future – that people can and do overcome the internal and external challenges, barriers, and obstacles that confront them.

- Recovery is person-driven: Self-determination and self-direction are the foundations for recovery as individuals define their own life goals and design their unique path(s).

- Recovery occurs via many pathways: Individuals are unique with distinct needs, strengths, preferences, goals, cultures, and backgrounds, including trauma experiences that affect and determine their pathway(s) to recovery. Abstinence is the safest approach for those with substance abuse disorders (however, is not the only way).

- Recovery is holistic: Recovery encompasses an individual's whole life, including mind, body, spirit, and community. The array of services and supports available should be integrated and coordinated.

- Recovery is supported by peers and allies: Mutual support and mutual aid groups, including the sharing of experiential knowledge and skills, as well as social learning, play an invaluable role in recovery.

- Recovery is supported through relationship and social networks: An important factor in the recovery process is the presence and involvement of people who believe in the person's ability to recover; who offer hope, support, and encouragement; and who also suggest strategies and resources for change.

- Recovery is culturally-based and influenced: Culture and cultural background in all of its diverse representations, including values, traditions, and beliefs, all of which determine a person's journey in recovery and ultimately their stability.

- Recovery is supported by addressing trauma: Services and supports should be trauma-informed to foster safety (physical and emotional) and trust, as well as promote choice, empowerment, and collaboration.

- Recovery involves individual, family, and community strengths and responsibility: Individuals, families, and communities have strengths and resources that serve as a foundation for recovery.

- Recovery is based on respect: Community, systems, and societal acceptance and appreciation for people affected by mental health and substance abuse problems – including protecting their rights and eliminating discrimination – are crucial in achieving recovery.

*For further detailed information about recovery or if you have questions please contact me (Eddie Olivas) at: EOlivas@ enduringhopecounseling.com

Made in the USA
Lexington, KY
11 April 2017